OLD BOOTS

REFLECTIONS ON COMING TO THE LAST BEND IN THE ROAD

OLD BOOTS

REFLECTIONS ON COMING TO THE LAST BEND IN THE ROAD

By

John Reynolds

Photographs by
Mary Spering and John Reynolds

Key Literary Concepts
Washington

OLD BOOTS

REFLECTIONS ON COMING TO THE LAST BEND
IN THE ROAD

Copyright © by John Reynolds

All rights reserved. No part of this book may be reproduced by any means, graphic, electronic or mechanical, including photocopying, recording, taping or by any information storage retrieval system without written permission of the publisher except in the case of brief quotations embodied in critical articles or reviews.

For information, address
Key Literary Concepts, P O Box 925
Vaughn, WA 98394

Printed in the United States of America

Reynolds, John
OLD BOOTS
REFLECTIONS ON COMING TO THE LAST BEND
IN THE ROAD

Library of Congress Control Number 2013940641

ISBN 978-0-9816065-8-3

Dedication

To Charles, for his unfailing support and encouragement

Acknowledgements

As a business writer, I had never seriously considered poetry until Melissa Haertsch, Betty Bryden and Tom Canouse of the Butternut Gallery in Montrose, PA created a venue for poets and invited me to be a part of it. My thanks to them also for pairing me with Mary Spering, whose photographs enhance the pages of this book.

I would also like to thank Jerry and Pam Libstaff of Watermark Writers for inspiriting fledgling poets like me and making this book happen.

INTRODUCTION

We have left undone those things which we ought to have done; and we have done those things which we ought not to have done. **Book of Common Prayer**,

Yes," said Deep Thought [the computer]. "Life, the Universe, and Everything. There is an answer. But, I'll have to think about it."

...

Fook glanced impatiently at his watch.

"How long?" he said.

"Seven and a half million years," said Deep Thought.

Lunkwill and Fook blinked at each other.

"Seven and a half million years...!" they cried in chorus.

"Yes," declaimed Deep Thought, "I said I'd have to think about it, didn't I?

[Douglas Adams, *The Hitchhiker's Guide to the Galaxy*][1]

None of us has seven and a half million years to ponder "life, the universe, and everything." What each of us has is but one lifetime to reflect on life, how things have gone so far, and what the future may hold in store.

For those as fortunate as I to have reached the age of sixty-five, that reflection may take on an added prominence. On the one hand, with careers behind us we have more hours in the day to devote to it. On the other hand, we are more conscious of our looming mortality and realize that we have fewer days to devote to the task.

And so we spend more time thinking, engaging in retrospection about the experiences we have had in our lives; in introspection about those experiences, good and bad, and what those experiences have taught us; and in projection – planning for our last decade or so of our lives and the most fulfilling use of the time we have left.

This book of poems is my way of reflecting on my life so far and what lies ahead.

Life is what happens while you are busy making other plans.
John Lennon

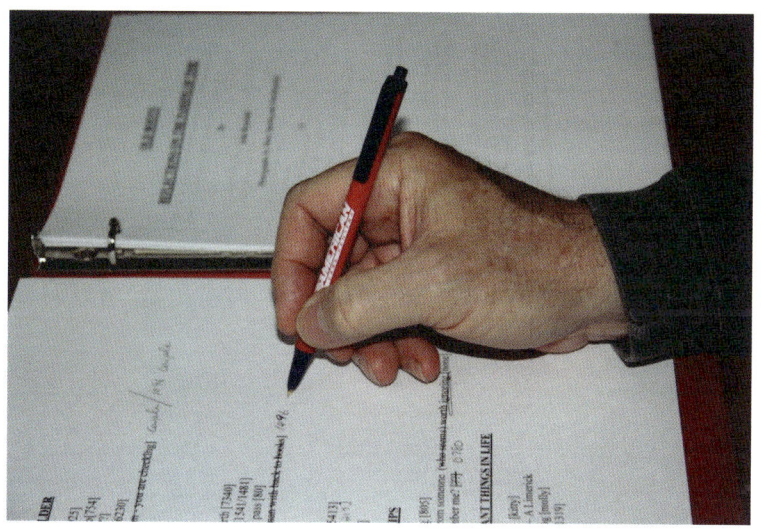

But first, some words on my approach:

<u>Poems that rhyme</u>

I fondly can recall a time
When poems were supposed to rhyme

An age when words were made to sing
And send the heart a-wandering

And more than that, they had a theme
Contained within the rhyming scheme

Now poems that are up to date
Demand I free associate

A feeling here, a vision there
Random thoughts from everywhere

Strung together end to end
No hint of what the words portend

But I'm old fashioned in my way
In how I form my word array

To me there is no greater crime
Than poesy whose words don't sound the same.

Table of Contents

ON GROWING OLDER

Old Boots	5
One year to go	6
One by one	8
Perspectives	10
Water	12
Green	14

ON WISDOM

What if	17
Heaven on Earth	18
Side by Side	19
This too shall pass	20
Is he right?	22

ON SUCCESS

Without me	24
Obscurity	25
Regret	26

ON RELATIONSHIPS

Almost Spring	28
Life lessons from someone (who seems) worth ignoring	29
Do you remember me?	31

ON THE IMPORTANT THINGS IN LIFE

Ode to my cat	34
Kitty-litterate – A Limerick	35
Little white dog	36
Ice Cream	38
Stuff	39

ON GROWING OLDER

Beware of all enterprises that require a new set of clothes.
Henry David Thoreau

Old Boots

The empty box lies on the floor
Marked "Workboots, Brown, Size 10"
They have the smell and feel of new
I try them on again

To me they feel more than a bit
Uncomfortable and strange
Is that not how it always is
When we are faced with change

I know that it would take some time
For me to break them in
Until the day they make peace with
The tired old feet within

My old boots on the floor show wounds
From campaigns they've been through
The heels are worn, the leather scarred
The laces are frayed, too

But like old friends they're comfortable
They let me have my way
They make no new demands of me
Their time is yesterday

There is a choice we all must make
As seasons come and go
Embrace the new and untried thing
Or stick with what we know

As I've grown old the shiny new
Intrigues me less each day
The time-worn still has much to tell
And active parts to play

I put my new boots in their box
And slip on my old friends
I think they're fit enough to last
Til my life's journey ends

***Millions long for immortality who don't know
what to do with themselves on a rainy Sunday
afternoon.*** **Susan Ertz**

One year to go

Suppose I knew for certain I had just one year to go
What would I change about my life – in truth I do not know

Would I race to finish projects I'd only just begun
Or make a new list of to-dos, of things I wish I'd done

I might indulge my chocolate muse and eat to overfill
Or possibly Terpsichore and samba in Brazil

There's Everest I've yet to climb, the Channel yet to swim
A thousand sights to choose among before my eyes grow dim

But might that be a bit too much to squeeze into one year
Perhaps I'd make a shorter list, of persons I hold dear

Family and special friends and others I most cherish
Who'd give me aid and comfort when came my day to perish

But I know just because a person means a lot to me
There's no assurance I can count on reciprocity

What if I thought my friends might wish to witness my demise
And then found out to my regret they all thought otherwise

The more I think of how I'd spend my last 300 days
The more my mental processes become a senseless haze

It might be best to have no plan and simply slip away
I've given this a lot of thought, but still I cannot say

I guess that when it comes to finding out just when I'll go
My ultimate conclusion is: it's better not to know

A friend who dies, it's something of you who dies.
Gustave Flaubert

<u>One by one</u>

Last night my cousin called to say

Her sister had just passed away

Now she is left, just one of three

Girls born into her family

I count on fingers those who've died

With whom I grew up side by side

And then I start to call to mind

Each one of those I've left behind

Each loss of a familiar face

Makes my small world a smaller place

So I'm aware from year to year

Of my diminished social sphere

It's not that I do not have new

Associates to help me through

But new acquaintance can't contend
With feelings for a lifelong friend
Nor fondness for a favored kin
Who walked the same world I walked in
But though they are not here today
I will not let them fade away
For each such passing, I instead
Create a place inside my head
Composed of friends and family
No longer on this earth with me
Where each corporal refugee
Assumes an immortality
Then thankful I can always be
That they can travel on with me

The windows of my soul I throw wide open to the sun.
Whittier

__Perspectives__

I woke up to the faintest glow
Through windows specked with flakes of snow

The dim first gleam of early dawn
Revealed pale shapes to ponder on

With eyes half open I could see
A shadow world held out to me

Then as the sun moved overhead
I saw a wider world instead

Beyond the grass and o'er the trees
Were endless possibilities

A universe of choices lay
Outside my window on that day

But overwhelmed by all in view
I froze, unsure of what to do

Then chose the safety of my cell
And clung to spaces I knew well

Adventure loomed beyond my reach
But my glass wall I would not breach

A small black bird, wings tipped with red
Peered in at me and cocked its head

How small the room he saw inside
How different from where birds reside

Where all I saw beyond my sill
Was his to wander in at will

Two aspects from points very near
But how distinct, the there from here

His interest in me having gone
He spread his wings and hastened on

The sun resumed its westward flight
And distant realms blinked out of sight

The options of the early day
Grew faint and then dissolved away

By evening shadows had returned
No wider world could be discerned

When darkness fell all I could see
Was my face looking back at me

My window was a looking glass
Reflecting what had come to pass

While I had seen what could have been
My reticence had held me in

The openings that came my way
Had faded like the light of day

I drew the curtains, went to bed
The chances missed still in my head

My eyes closed, I looked back upon
A life unlived, a life forgone

Life in us is like the water in a river. - **Henry David Thoreau**

Let the most absent-minded of men be plunged in his deepest reveries--stand that man on his legs, set his feet a-going, and he will infallibly lead you to water, if water there be in all that region. Should you ever be athirst in the great American desert, try this experiment, if your caravan happen to be supplied with a metaphysical professor. Yes, as every one knows, meditation and water are wedded for ever. **Herman Melville,** *Moby Dick*

Water

The mists of early spring recall
The faint beginnings of it all
Before the drops began to fall
My world was strange and new

The mist gave way to gentle rain
Repeating as a soft refrain
Like simple lessons on my brain
The child in me emerged

Each shower that ensued brought me
The joy of fresh discovery
My early days I came to see
Were carefree and serene

But then a flood washed over me
And tossed about an angry sea
Unsure where I was meant to be
I drifted with the tide

Then stepped out on a distant shore
Not unlike one I'd seen before
But it was rich and offered more
From there I made my way

The summer of my years were warm
But for the passing thunderstorm
How readily did I conform
To adulthood's demands

In time the waters slowed until
They almost were completely still
All quiet neath December's chill
Reflecting skies of gray

The world's become all whiteness now
as winter takes a frosty bow
it seems a miracle somehow
that I have come so far

Now I stand mid ice and snow
Aware that I've not long to go
I look back at the ebb and flow
That brought me to this place

From April rain to frozen lake
How like the course we all must take
From waking breath to solemn wake
From source to river's end

My cup refilled with each advance
One day with pain, the next romance
Were I to have a second chance
I'd come this way again

Man has been endowed with reason, with the power to create, so that he can add to what he's been given. But up to now he hasn't been a creator, only a destroyer. Forests keep disappearing, rivers dry up, wild life's become extinct, the climate's ruined and the land grows poorer and uglier every day. ~**Anton Chekhov, Uncle Vanya**

Green

I climbed up high where I could see
Miles of green in front of me

I cocked my head from side to side
And saw the green was vast and wide

Off to the left a streak of brown
Defined the road that led to town

And on my right I saw the gleam
Reflecting off a rushing stream

But I knew that there was no stream
And no dirt road, twas all a dream

My memory's creation of
A landscape I did one time love

A spectacle of shades of green
I left behind at age thirteen

Five decades later I return
Retrace my steps and sadly learn

That brown has given way to black
A paved and stubby cul-de-sac

And green space these days comes in spots
The size of acre building lots

The little stream can now be found
In plastic pipe deep underground

How readily did man demean
How better had he left it green

In no place can I clearer see
How good my childhood was for me

By that remark I simply mean
I grew up when the world was green

ON WISDOM

Christianity, if false, is of no importance, and if true, of infinite importance. The only thing it cannot be is moderately important. **C.S. Lewis**

What if...

When I was seventeen I knew
as much as one could know
I knew what things I should
oppose and what things I was pro

How wiser I than older men whose blindness was quite clear
Whose simple faith in god and country discomposed my ear

But then my first gray hairs appeared and caused me to reflect
Might there be something to this faith I earnestly reject?

Decades passed, more doubts arose, my certainties abated
What if, I wondered, they were right, and better times awaited

What if there is an afterlife, a heaven and a hell
What if what lies beyond is more than science can foretell

The peaceful smiles of men of faith can rightly give one pause
They seem to sense within what counts and do not seek the cause

I cannot say I know for sure what lies beyond death's curtain
But will I simply cease to be; these days I'm not so certain.

***Aim at heaven and you will get earth thrown in.
Aim at earth and you get neither.* C.S. Lewis**

Heaven on Earth

I've often pondered what was meant
When someone said "she's heaven-sent".

Was heaven both a place to start
And final stop for pure of heart

How curious it seemed to me
This place, both source and destiny.

In come those souls devoid of sin
But what of us whose lives begin

On earth, when from a worldly mold
A new life joins the human fold?

So have we here a two-way street
With passing souls that never meet?

Or is it more like out and in –
A heavenly recycling bin?

I guess I just must wait and see
If heaven be the end of me.

Nothing's beautiful from every point of view. **Horace**

Side by side

The colors surely are the same
A tree is still a tree

The people she sees walking by
Should look the same to me

And yet the world that she beholds
Is not the same as mine

What I regard as commonplace
She translates as a sign

A sign that means that all is good
Or maybe all's not well

A sign that tells her "move along"
When I might sit a spell

What she regards as timeless art
I see as pointless spatter

I love the sound of modern jazz
To her it's all just clatter

And that's just two perspectives on
A world that we two share

Imagine then just how diverse
The other views out there

A world of seven billion souls
With fourteen billion eyes

That each one sees things dirrerently
Should come as no surprise

Nor is it any wonder that
When we want something more

Than others are prepared to cede
Disputes can lead to war

Little wars like family feuds
Or big ones like divorce

Or great big ones like World War II
That change a nation's course

Confronting those who disagree
Is what all people do

It matters not how large the crowd
It takes no more than two

This too shall pass
Sufi Proverb

This too shall pass

    Just why the Roman Empire fell historians still debate
    Why did the Romans reach a peak and then disintegrate

    The rationales range far and wide and some are very clever
    Perhaps a simpler rule applies: that "nothing lasts forever"

    What happened to the Maya and Atlantis and the Khmer
    Can happen somewhere any time; it's happening right here

    The rule applies to everything, and not just mighty nations
    It's just as true for families and faiths and corporations

    It's not just floods or asteroids or failure to adapt
    That causes human packaging to one day come unwrapped

    Society's a fragile thing regardless of its size
    And mankind has a fatal flaw and there the problem lies

To reconcile what's good for me with what is good for us
For even those who make the try it's still quite arduous

And what seems good for us right now may hurt us in the end
While we enjoy the ride we're on we can't see round the bend

It doesn't seem to matter just how good things are today
The best of times seem to contain the seeds of their decay

The world has always been this way and always will, I guess
We learn each generation "nothing fails quite like success"

Nothing is so firmly believed as what we least know. **Montaigne**

It ain't what you don't know that gets you into trouble. It's what you know for sure that just ain't so. **Mark Twain.**

Is he right?

Once he

What is this thing he's on about
Of which he shows no hint of doubt

His passion fuels a loud tirade
That makes me just a bit afraid

That words might turn to violence
Immune to pleas for common sense

His fury turns on those that he
Suspects might dare to disagree

What use endeavors to inform
If but to fuel a thunderstorm

Politics, faith and football teams
He knows it all, or so it seems

No scholarship supports his stance
His research is a casual glance

He sees no need to check his facts
once he decides which team he backs

But such unquestioned loyalty		The know-nothing, both left and right
Displaces his integrity			Knows nothing more than to incite

The better man is someone who
Begins by asking "Is it true?"

22

ON SUCCESS

He is a modest little man with much to be modest about.
Winston Churchill

Without me

Suppose I went to sleep one day and then did not awake
I wonder in the scheme of things what difference that would make

How would the friends and kin of mine experience the loss
Would they regard my simple gifts as so much applesauce

And what if my departure had occurred some years ago
Would history have changed its course is what I want to know

Whatever would the world be like were I to disappear
However would it muddle through were I no longer here

Sometimes I fantasize and think the sun would cease to shine
But in reality I know the world would be just fine

My life's too unaccomplished to have etched a timeless mark
No famous name, no lasting fame, no statue in the park

In history's grand atlas I don't even rate a dot
But is there still a tiny chance that I won't be forgot?
                Afraid not!

When all else fails, immortality may be achieved through a spectacular failure. **J. Kenneth Galbraith**

<u>Obscurity</u>

I may have been but twenty when it first occurred to me
My future did not hold a date with immortality

No moon walks, cancer cure and not a single Nobel Prize
Nothing to distinguish me in my fellow beings' eyes

There may be time remaining yet to change the path of fate
To seize the day, to strike it rich, accomplish something great

But fickle fate has lots to say on who achieves success
Awarding some with more, and others with a whole lot less

And lasting fame attends not just to those the masses hail
 It also fixes firmly to the rest of us who fail

Like Custer, Hannibal. .. Napoleon at Waterloo
Then there's the Edsel and Titanic - just to name a few

So if a quest for greatness also risks calamity
How shrewd of me to play it safe and choose obscurity

In 20 years you will be more disappointed by what you didn't do than by what you did. **Mark Twain.**

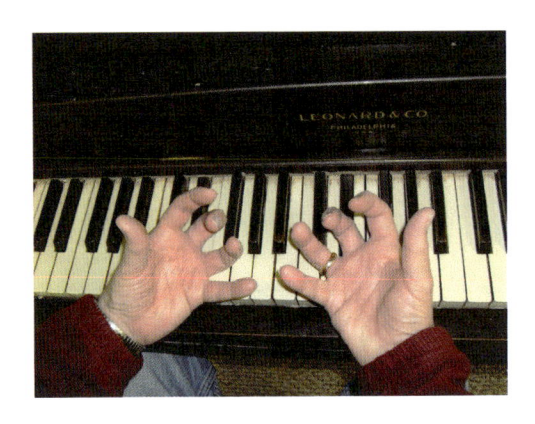

<u>Regret</u>

Of all the things I might have done
I hold regret for only one

I wish I'd been a pianist
Like Chopin, Cliburn or Franz Liszt

In my fantasies I'd dash off
A prelude from Rachmaninoff

Romance the keys and celebrate 'em
And improvise just like Art Tatum

Melody would flow most freely
I'd grin and say "It's nothing really".

Each night I rehearse every
Impracticable reverie

But I awake and clearly see
Each one's impossibility

It's not as if I didn't try
My music muse to satisfy

It's just I've learned my sole redeeming
Talent is a knack for dreaming.

ON RELATIONSHIPS

One thing I remember :
Spring came on forever,
Spring came on forever…
    Vachel Lindsay

Almost Spring…an almost love song

Before the first snowdrop appears
From specks of snow white souvenirs
Of winter's one last icy sting
That is when it's almost spring.

It's not quite cold, but not yet green
The days are kind of in between
The birds aren't sure what songs to sing
When the time is almost spring.

I find that I'm of two minds, too.
I'm lacking in direction.
I simply don't know what to do
In matters of affection.

There's someone I am thinking of.
Is it too soon to talk of love?
My heart is still meandering
When it's almost spring.

[slow]
I'll chance romance and have my fling…
    When at last…it's finally…Spring!

Appearances often are deceiving **AESOP**

Beware as long as you live, of judging people by appearances
Jean de la Fontaine

Life lessons from someone (who seems) worth ignoring

It wasn't just his giant size that caught my eye at first
The fit and color of his clothes displayed him at his worst

His scraggly beard and unkempt hair obscured a brooding face
And all in all I'd seen enough to leave him in his place

The place he chose was by himself beside the kitchen door
Where he pursued obscurity as part of the décor

The other guests ignored this man and left him on his own
And I resolved to do the same and leave the man alone

What could this creature have to say, what knowledge to impart
I turned and joined the "smarter" set who dressed and looked the part

An hour went by, by then I knew what movies I should see,
And who was who and what was what and how the world should be

The giant had maintained his stead and looked quite far away
Was there the slightest chance, I thought, he'd anything to say.

Soon boredom overcame me and I left the noisy swarm
I slowly made my way to him and touched him on the arm

At first he seemed surprised by me and slowly turned to stare
Why had I not kept to my plan and left him standing there.

"Forgive me if I seem detached," he said and smiled at me
"I'm working on a problem with a piece by Debussy."

He shook my hand and asked me for my thoughts on harmony
We talked composers old and new, and concerts he might see

He talked of Brahms and Borodin, Picasso and Van Gogh
And held forth on a world of things I simply did not know.

And what an education I obtained for free that night
I learned that first impressions are as often wrong as right

And here this awkward man held neither title nor degree
Though I held more than one of both, this man now tutored me.

Appearances can well deceive, and beauty can conceal
A want of substance from within, a lack of what is real

Likewise a lack of polish and a look distinctly odd
Can often hide a noble soul behind a strange façade

My friend, I now can call him that, imbued me with this sense
And I have made more real friends since I learned the difference

Remember me with smiles and laughter, for that is how I will remember you all. If you can only remember me with tears, then don't remember me at all. **Laura Ingalls Wilder**

No memory of having starred Atones for later disregard
Robert Frost *Provide, Provide*

Do you remember me?

Sometimes I like to reminisce
On when you gave me my first kiss
The thing I want to know is this
Do you remember me?

And you to whom I gave my heart
Until the draft forced us apart
And passion we could not restart
Do you remember me?

The best friend from my grade school days
My co-stars from my high school plays
Who shaped my life so many ways
Do you remember me?

To all of you I owe a debt
But I would feel sincere regret
If all of you I can't forget
Do not remember me.

ON THE IMPORTANT THINGS IN LIFE

Time spent with cats is never wasted. **Sigmund Freud**

Ode to my Cat

My little cat won't go away
She makes demands ten times a day

Sometimes she's hungry, wants to eat
Fresh tuna is her special treat

But other times she wants a nap
And wants it on a nice warm lap

Her favorite time to be with me
Is when I watch my old TV

She moves from couch to lap to chest
Til she decides which spot feels best

Then settles in to have her snooze
Which lasts up to the late night news

We have a bond, my cat and I
As we both watch the years go by

That bond I've shared with six before
I've time left for at least one more

Each one a comfort and a friend
Through my existence, first to end.

And when the world's too close around
And life's vicissitudes confound

There's no more soothing balm than that
of a loving, purring pussy cat.

Kitty Litter-ate – A Limerick

My cat is one literate kitty
Regarded by all as quite witty
   Her powers of prose
   Exceed mine, goodness knows
That's why she chose to
   author this ditty

My goal in life is to be as good of a person my dog already thinks I am.
~**Author Unknown**

Little White Dog

Each day there is a dialogue
Between me and my small white dog

She lets me know what lurks outside
And when it's time to take a ride

Her face reflects concern when she
Sees that something's bothering me

And lights up like the Great White Way
When I agree it's time to play

Sometimes I think she reads my mind
Though thinking is beyond her kind

At least that's what my friends hold true
A dog will walk along with you

And sit and stay and fetch a ball
Obey commands, but that is all

But I'm convinced that they're all wrong
My dog does more than tag along

She mirrors my emotive states
My feelings she anticipates

A doppelganger clothed in fur
I'd say she's as much "us" as "her"

Without ice cream life and fame are meaningless
Unknown

Ice Cream

Were I marooned on an atoll ring
Where I could take a single thing
I know for sure what I would bring
My choice would be ice cream

Or were I on a stellar trek
To kill time I'd say "what the heck!"
And head down to the holodeck
For mounds of good ice cream

When God created things his way
He didn't waste the seventh day
I think you could have heard him say
" I feel like some ice cream."

In real life as I antiquate
And even though I'm overweight
I find I do not hesitate
To ask for more ice cream

So when life's woes you can't endure
Or you are feeling insecure
May I suggest the perfect cure
Go fill up on ice cream

A house is just a pile of stuff with a cover on it.
George Carlin

Stuff

If I had ever thought of it I never would have thunk
That any single person could acquire such piles of junk

Some scraps of wood and power tools that never felt my hand
Electric things I cannot bring my mind to understand

And shoes and books and pictures and huge mounds of bric-a-brac
That seem to breed and grow too big for one man to attack

My friend tells me my hopeless mess is not exactly trash
And that a little marketing might turn it into cash

But that would take an awful lot of organizing skill
Or someone quite unlike myself with lots of time to kill

I'll turn my back and look away and let it reproduce
And print up cards that say "antiques" – how's that for an excuse?

John Reynolds is a Free-lance writer who specializes in business writing about insurance and finance. He wanders into nonfiction, children's writing, poetry and song lyrics when time permits. John lives in New Miford, PA.

Mary Spering, a retired educator, and lifelong resident of Dimock, PA, is rarely without her camera and focuses on subjects ranging from trees and plants to frogs, dragonflies and grandchildren. She loves to capture the beauty of nature and can happily spend many an hour "chasing flowers" or looking for another pastoral scene. Mary belongs to an e-mail photography group with members in Pennsylvania, Connecticut and Montana.

[1]"The More Than Complete Hitchhiker's Guide"
by Douglas Adams, Wings Books (NY) 1989

Photos:

By Mary Spering

Introduction	
Old Boots	Pg 5
One Year ago	Pg 6
One by One	Pg 8
Perspectives	Pg 10
Water	Pg 12
Green	Pg 14
What if	Pg 17
Heaven on Earth	Pg 18
Side by Side	Pg 19
This too shall pass	Pg 20
Is he right	Pg 22
Without me	Pg 24
Obscurity	Pg 25
Almost Spring	Pg 28
Do you remember	Pg 31
Ice Cream	Pg 38

By John Reynolds

Regret	Pg 26
Kitty Litter-ate	Pg 35
Little White Dog	Pg 36
Stuff	Pg 39

Made in the USA
Lexington, KY
10 February 2014